Tales

LADY IN GREY

with a touch of Scarlet

Lt.-Col. R. Sutton

QARANC (Rtd) ARRC

BARGATE BOOKS

© Rosemary Sutton 2007
Tales of a Lady in Grey with a touch of Scarlet

ISBN   978-0-9555945-0-2

Published by Bargate Books
Bargate House
Tuesley Lane
Godalming
Surrey
GU7 1SB

The right of Rosemary Sutton to be identified as the author of this work has been asserted by her in accordance with the Copyright, Designs and Patents Act 1988.

A CIP catalogue record of this book
can be obtained from the British Library.

Designed & produced by:
The Better Book Company Ltd
Forum House
Stirling Road
Chichester
West Sussex
PO19 7DN

Printed in England

Rosemary Sutton

This book is dedicated to my parents

FLORENCE & EDWARD SUTTON

CONTENTS

1   Family History..1

2   Becoming a Nurse 6

3   Initiation into the Army 13

4   Nursing for the Army 16

5   Nursing Overseas

     Egypt 21

     Malta...25

6   Neurosurgery Training 30

7   Two years in Sierra Leone.............................34

8   Tour in Kenya..52

9   Tour in Berlin 57

10   Marjorie..67

11   WRAC Centre Guildford 69

12   Retirement 70

I wish to acknowledge the assistance given to me
in producing this book by:

JOAN GARWOOD

LOUISE LA CROIX

MALCOLM & DENISE BRUNNING

1

Family History

I was born on 5 February 1917 in Withyham, West Sussex. It was very snowy and I was overdue so my poor father was forced to be absent without leave from the Great War if he was to be present for my arrival. Fortunately when he returned to France, in the compassionate circumstances, he was only deducted one week's pay. My maternal grandmother, a midwife who had trained at the Louise Margaret Hospital, Aldershot, was there to assist with my birth. Although she didn't actually deliver me, it was fortunate that she was around as I was quite a poorly baby and needed to be resuscitated.

Prior to training as a midwife, my grandmother, Elizabeth (maiden name Carter) was a professional nanny in London and that is where she met my grandfather. I know that she walked through Hyde Park with her charges regularly. My grandfather, Daniel Heath was in the Royal Horse Artillery based nearby at Wellington Barracks at the time. Elizabeth was young, attractive and vivacious and I imagine she caught Daniel's eye while out and about in the park. They got talking and one thing led to another. This would have been about the mid 1800s and there was still quite a well-established class divide. My grandfather was from quite a well-to-do family. They hailed from Burslem in Staffordshire and had made their fortune in property. I have always had the impression that his family considered my grandfather a wayward son. Normally, someone of his social standing would have entered the Army at officer rank. He was probably put in the Army in an effort to sort him out and he joined up at Private rank. Nonetheless he must have thrived in the Army for he rose to the rank of Sergeant in a relatively short space of time.

The Heaths it seems, felt that their Daniel had married beneath him and wouldn't have anything to do with his new wife or subsequent children. The full nature of this attitude came to light when the time came that my grandmother was put in dire need.

At this time Britain was taking over in Egypt in an attempt to protect their route to India from both the French and the Russian threat. My grandfather was posted to Egypt (Cazanal barracks) during the 1880s and this may have precipitated the marriage. While in Egypt my mother, Florence, and my uncle, also Daniel, were born. While posted in Egypt my grandfather was sent south to Sudan to aid Major General Gordon during the defence of Khartoum against the rebels there. In 1884 Britain was forced to intervene in Sudan where the Egyptian forces were being brutally massacred by religion-fuelled rebels. They sent Gordon to Khartoum to evacuate the Egyptian forces. Khartoum came under siege from the Sudanese rebels within the month and Gordon was killed along with many other defenders. The British relief force survivors of the battle, including my grandfather, returned to Cairo.

Having survived his mission in Sudan my grandfather was returned to Egypt. However, there was a bizarre and ultimately fatal incident during Ramadan that led to my grandfather being stabbed to death. My grandfather had a dog as a pet. For some unfathomable reason his batman looked after his uniform and quarters etc., a local man, decided that he wanted the dog and he stabbed my grandfather to death. My own, subsequent, experiences of Ramadan, have revealed that the people celebrating this religious occasion can behave very strangely indeed. People you know and have worked with, who are normally friendly and reliable can behave badly, violently or sometimes embarrassingly be amorous. Perhaps it is a heady combination of drugs, hunger and the promise that forgiveness will be forthcoming if the sinner performs his rituals rigorously during this festival.

Clearly, my grandmother was now left in a grave situation. With her two small children, aged 5 and 2 years old, she returned to England where she stayed with relatives in Balden Oxfordshire. In an effort to keep her family together, she approached he father-in-law Sir James Heath for assistance. He offered to take her children from her and pay for them to be educated but in return she must never see them again! Of course there was no question, her answer was an emphatic 'No!'

She was forced to return to work as a nanny to provide for her family. As nannies were live-in she left my mother (Florence) with an aunt to look after her and my uncle (Daniel) was sent to the Duke of York boarding school where he stayed until he joined his father's regiment, The Royal Horse Artillery, around the turn of the century.

During his tenure with the Royal Horse Artillery, my Uncle Daniel fought in the First World War. He was very badly wounded, lost a leg and nearly died. Apparently, an explosion went off very close to him and he was subsequently left with many shrapnel wounds. He later married but sadly, due to his injuries, he was unable to have children. As a child I was very fond of Uncle Dan. I can remember being very worried about a lump on his head. He told me not to worry that it was something that got put there during the war and it would in time work its way out and it did.

Due to his disabilities, the Army trained him in boot repair to give him a skill for civilian life. He set up his own business and opened a shop repairing shoes in Withyham near my gran's house. Initially, after leaving the Army, he lived with gran but when he met and married a local girl he moved into his own home.

My father Edward Sutton was in the Royal Enniskillen Fusiliers and he stayed in the army until the end of the First

World War. My parents decided they would like to live in the countryside and so my father took a job as manager of a farm in Merrow, Guildford. He continued in this career all his life.

I don't know much about my father's family, the Suttons, but he came from quite a large family. His father worked for the railway. My paternal grandmother died and my grandfather married a second time to a woman with children so making a huge family. I understand my father and his brothers were always getting into mischief.

My father and his elder brother Harry emigrated to Canada where they bought a smallholding. My father's job there was a backwoodsman which was quite lucrative. He must have been homesick for he made the trip from the woods into Toronto three times with the intention of returning to England. However, each time he went to Toronto he got distracted by the attractions of the city, blew all his money, forcing him to return to his job in the woods. Eventually, he made the return journey to England where he met and married my mother. My mother refused to emigrate to Canada and so they stayed in England.

I did get to know one of my father's younger brothers, Edwin (Ned). He had been in the Royal Navy but jumped ship in Australia and remained there for his life. He actually became quite famous in the field of entomology and owned a fruit plantation in the outback of Queensland. My Uncle Ned had done quite a bit of research into the Sutton family history and he wrote to me when I was travelling with the Army. He contacted me when I was in Africa, as he wanted a particular type of beetle that is native there. I duly sent him some samples.

He told me many interesting stories including one about a Sutton ancestor who had been in the Navy with Drake and ended up being buried in Zanzibar. Uncle Ned was quite an interesting man and he had contacts at The British Museum London. They have a rare beetle on display there collected and sent to them by my uncle.

I have been led to believe there is a connection between the Sutton family and Charterhouse School. I think they may have been benefactors and given money to the school during its infancy in London before it moved to Godalming in Surrey.

I also got to know one of my cousins from my father's side. His name was Jeffrey Westbrook and he was my father's sister's son. When my aunt visited with Jeff for the first time I was about ten years old and he was about fourteen. We met several times during the latter part of the war (WWII) by which time Jeff had joined up and was in the Grenadiers. His family lived in Wallingford and I remember visiting with them when Jeff was on leave. He appeared very glamorous to me and we started to write to each other especially after he was sent to France. Eventually he proposed to me and we even looked into whether we could legally marry. I accepted his proposal and shortly after that he was posted to the Sahara as a Desert Rat. By the time the war ended I had my wedding dress ready. Everyone was very happy with the arrangement but then my mother died and Jeff had trouble settling into civilian life. Although he was a Sergeant in the Army he had no trade and couldn't find a job. At that point in our lives we found that we had very little in common and decided to call off the wedding. It was all very amiable and I felt very strongly that I had made the right decision. Some time later he did marry and I heard he had three sons. I hoped that he had a happy life.

After my parents had passed away I was left pretty much without close family. My mother had a second pregnancy but it had ended in miscarriage (it was a boy) and I had no close cousins. The only relatives were cousins of my mother and there must have been cousins from my father's side.

2

Becoming a Nurse

Growing up, I hated school but loved nature and enjoyed helping my father around the farm. I learned how to milk cows and loved it! Into adulthood, I continued living with my parents, working on the farm until my mother became very ill. She nearly died. It turned out she had a dermoid cyst and had to undergo a hysterectomy. The nurse who looked after her was very kind to my mother and they became close friends. Even after my mother returned home from hospital they stayed in close contact and this nurse was invited to any party or family gathering that there was. I guess I rather resented this relationship between my mother and this nurse. However, it inspired me to become a nurse.

Too young to train I became a resident nursing assistant at Weybridge Cottage Hospital. When I was old enough I left to undertake my nursing training at Mayday Hospital, Croydon and was based there throughout the Second World War.

During this time, the whole of the Croydon area was regularly bombed and we saw a lot of bomb victims at the hospital. In fact the hospital itself was actually hit once. A doctor and two patients were killed during this attack but it could have been much worse. The bomb that hit, fell into the lift-shaft and missed the more populated zones of the hospital.

Whilst at Croydon, food was rationed for us like everyone else. I was always hungry and could never get enough to eat. The grounds of the hospital had been temporarily turned over to locals to grow vegetables. One evening, in desperation, I stole into the vegetable plot and unearthed some potatoes.

Unfortunately a man came along but he didn't see me. I dropped to the ground and hid in the potato patch until he went away. I cooked the potatoes for my supper, they were very nice but I'd learned my lesson and didn't attempt a repeat!

Another time when all the hospital staff had sat down to a supper of fish and chips from the hospital kitchen, someone found a deep fried mouse in amongst the chips! I was called upon by the group (for some reason I was always made the ringleader) to report the find to Matron. She took me to one side and informed me that the boiling fat of chip oil was very hot so the mouse was sterile and therefore we shouldn't worry!

Every third day I did a shift on the Casualty ward and I can remember one incident that sticks in my mind. There had been a bombing raid in the area and an old lady was brought into Casualty during my shift. She was in a right state. She was swearing at everyone and completely hysterical. I was sent to calm her down and find out where she was injured. It turned out that the injury was not on her person. She had been patiently saving her meat ration coupons to buy a Christmas joint and the whole lot had been blown up during the raid. She was inconsolable!

Another incident sticks in my mind. Again I was on shift after a particularly bad bombing raid. A buzz bomb had hit an evacuation centre which at the time was packed with civilians (mostly women and children) waiting to be rehoused or moved on to their evacuation home. There were many victims and a lot were children. One ward took in all casualties and each nurse on duty was assigned four stretchers each. As people were brought in they were assigned to a nurse and then the nurse decided with the doctor whether to patch them up and send them home, send them on to the main ward for further treatment or if they had died they were sent directly to the mortuary. I had a shift at the mortuary one of the nights and remember as clearly as if it were yesterday having to lay out a little four year-old boy. At first he seemed untouched, perfect, a beautiful little blond boy until I came to his head which had a hole in the top where a shard of wood had pierced his skull. It was extremely hard for me, all of it, but this particular event has always haunted me.

One night when I was on duty on the admissions ward during this particular raid, an old man covered in blood was brought in. I glared at the admission's officer when he assigned him to me because I was already up to my eyes in it and this looked like a particularly involved case. I said to the old man 'Dad, where are you hurting?' and he replied, 'I'm not hurt, love.' It turned out that it was not his blood but that of his mate who had been sleeping in the next bed at the evacuation centre. I cleaned him up and sent him on his way without so much as a scratch. It was like that, two people could be right next to each other, one would be blown to pieces and the other not a hair harmed. Quite hard to fathom really.

When I had leave from Croydon I went home to visit my parents. At that time they were living at Stilemans, Godalming where my father was the farm manager. Once, when I had two whole weeks at home I would help my father around the farm. He was concerned that the chickens were not laying, perhaps rats were stealing the eggs. So I took the .22 rifle and a book and sat up on watch in the trees above the chicken house for an afternoon. Late that afternoon I saw two soldiers scale the fence. Apparently some Canadian troops were billeted at the adjacent estate. They rifled through the chicken coop for eggs. They hadn't spotted me, so just as they were leaving with the eggs I fired a shot in the air. They dropped the eggs and scrambled back over the fence. I told my parents what had happened and we all thought it was hilarious.

Sometime later on a Canadian soldier called round at the house. He was looking to rent a room for a fellow soldier who had recently married whilst stationed in Somerset, and needed somewhere for his young wife to stay. She was a lovely girl and we gladly took her in but this is how they found out that it was I who had shot at them! They took it well and we became friends. Every time I was home on leave they arranged some transport to pick me up at the station and bring me home. We would socialise at the local pub, The Queen's Arms on the Brighton Road, and one of the soldiers, John, took a shine to me. When his friends realised that he was getting serious about me they took me to one side and warned me that John was a very kind, brave and serious man. I was to be careful not to break his heart. I was young and just wanted to have a good time. I didn't feel as strongly for John as he did about me and I still had hopes for Jeff at the time. Eventually they were all posted to France and John left his belongings with me to look after until he could return for them. He did come and visit once during a 48 hour leave but returned to France. I never heard from him again. There was nothing I could do about it, as I had no home address for him. I knew that he came from Longford Mills, Ontario and I wrote to him there hoping it was a small town and someone could get the letter to him. I didn't get a reply and so I assumed he was killed in action.

While I was still working at Croydon my mother became very ill again. I decided to resign so that I could look after her. Her doctors couldn't work out what was wrong with her and after about a month she was admitted to hospital. Looking after my father and visiting my mother in hospital was time consuming but I still needed to find a job. I took a job as Sister at the temporary hospital at Merrow (convalescent home for patients from the Royal Surrey County Hospital in Guildford). I stayed there for about a year until the end of the war. Tragically, my mother died during that time aged 53. She had had very bad arthritis and they treated her with injections of gold. I believe it was this that actually caused her death.

My father was very distressed and could no longer work. We decided to leave the farm and my father took on a less demanding job looking after a small herd of pedigree Dexter cows on an estate at Witley (Coat's the cotton people had a rare breeds collection at their estate). A small flat in Witley came with the job.

Meanwhile, as the war ended the convalescent hospital in Merrow closed and I got a position at the Royal Surrey, Farnham Road, Guildford as a junior Night Sister. This post was non-residential so I lived with my father and was able to keep an eye on him.

I was Night Sister with theatre duties at Farnham Road for about three years. During this time two cases stand out in my mind.

It was just after the war had ended and a little girl was admitted to my ward. She was gravely ill. At the handover with the Day Sister I was warned that I was in for a worrying night. What had happened was the little girl had been playing up on Stag Hill (near the unfinished Guildford Cathedral) with her younger brother and their dog. They came across a soldier who was almost certainly AWOL at the time. I do not know what transpired at the time but the soldier attacked and killed the dog and the boy and left the girl for dead. They found her and brought her to the hospital but she died that night from her injuries. The man was caught and I remember the press was all over the hospital. It was a very sad time. It would seem that the soldier was in need of psychiatric help possibly because of the horrors he had witnessed during the war.

On a slightly lighter note I can recall another memorable event from my time at Farnham Road. One night the police brought a man to the hospital. They had found him seemingly unconscious on the steps to the underground public toilets on North Street Guildford. The doctor on call was at the local pub celebrating his birthday and I had instructions to call the pub should I need him. Anyway the patient was brought in and I checked his vital signs but could not find anything obviously wrong with him. I called the pub to speak to the doctor and he instructed me to have him X-rayed by which time he would be back to examine him.

Meanwhile the police called me to ask me for a favour. They had checked out what they thought was his home address and found it to be incorrect. They wanted me to look through his pockets to see if there was another address. As my assistant nurse and I were doing this I found a gun in his pocket, at which point he suddenly woke up. He became very agitated and in the ensuing struggle the curtain screen got knocked over and all the patients on the ward woke up. I took the gun and locked it in the drug cabinet and called the police. They were extremely embarrassed at their blunder and sent someone over straight away. I could hear the bells all the way from North Street.

It transpired that the police had been chasing a burglar when they had found this unconscious man at the public toilets. They hadn't realised that they were one and the same man and when the chasing policemen started getting close to the burglar he played dead! The police were very sorry and chastened by the whole affair. They had put my staff, my patients and me in some danger. By way of an apology they sent me a gift of some bound books.

I worked the night shift (four on, three off) for three years whilst looking after my father. He became increasingly concerned about the toll it was all having on me and employed a housekeeper several times but each time it ended in disaster. He suggested that he could get a smaller place on his own so that I would be free to live my own life but I wasn't happy for him to be on his own.

Eventually, he asked me how I would feel if he was to get married again. Initially, I was a bit taken aback and asked him what he had been up to. I said, 'No one will want an old man, surely …' but he told me there might be someone. Somewhat surprised to say the least, I asked him who that might be. He explained that up at the estate where he worked they had a cook who was quite keen on him. I told him that in principle it was all right with me if it made him happy and arrangements were made for 'the proposal'. We saved up all our sweet coupons and we bought her a box of chocolates and my father asked cook out to dinner. When he arrived home after the date he asked me to get him a brandy 'She said yes!' he exclaimed. They duly got married and set up home together in Witley. This left me free to take a resident's job at the Royal Surrey County as Theatre Sister.

3

Initiation into the Army

My time in this post was fairly uneventful and after a while I decided I needed a challenge. My experiences as a nurse at Croydon during the war had influenced me enormously and I had considered joining the Army while the war was still underway, but my father, normally not a demonstrative man, insisted it would break my mother's heart so I had held off. I wanted to continue with my nursing but I wanted to serve and I wanted to travel. I now felt free to join up and applied to all three armed services. The Army was the first to respond. They called me up to the War Office for an interview and then I was sent to Millbank for a medical assessment. This was very thorough and part of the assessment included a physical appraisal called a 'PULLEAMS'. The purpose of this assessment was to match you to the appropriate role and rank. To be in the Queen Alexandra (QA) Royal Ancillary Nursing Corps I needed to score a 'P3'. After I took the paper the assessor called me in and told me 'It's no good I'm afraid, no matter what I do I can't seem to make you any less than a P4!' This was the score for a paratrooper! Needless to say I was passed good enough for the QARANC post.

The QAs started after Florence Nightingale, when Queen Alexandra took over the nursing of the military and called the Sisters the 'Queen Alexandra's Imperial Nursing Service'. The Sisters were known as the 'Ladies Attached to the Army'.

After World War II, when some Nursing Sisters were taken prisoner in the Far East by the Japanese and treated as civilians, it was decided to make them regular Army Officers.

13

This was because they were treated so cruelly, as were the soldiers, but without the rights of the soldiers. We are now known as 'Queen Alexandra's Royal Army Nursing Corps'. Recognised as officers, we now have to salute and understand and obey the Queen's Regulations and the Manual of Military Law. Queen Alexandra wanted her Sisters to have a little scarlet with their grey dresses and so it was that we were known as the 'Grey and Scarlets' by the men at the Front.

When I joined the QAs in February 1949 this was just before the changes to their status were being brought in. Initially, my rank under the old system was 'Subaltern'. This then changed to the equivalent at the time, which was Lieutenant.

On acceptance into the QAs I had to report to KEO Barracks at Mytchett for the new intake in February 1949. I was billeted with twelve other nurses and all I had to my name was a bed and a locker. This was a bit of a shock to the system. We had to share a few bathrooms not just between us twelve, but with all the other QAs 'in transit'. (At that time every QA returned to Mytchett both before and after each posting. After the war there were a lot of people at Mytchett, many of whom were leaving the Army for good.)

Reporting in to Mytchett for the first time I had to go to the admin office and give up my ration book. Whilst there I was confronted by a very attractive female QA officer. She had an orderly with her. I was always tall and, in those days, pale and thin also. She must have thought I was ill because she got the orderly to fetch me a chair and bade me sit down. When I explained I wasn't ill, she told the orderly to take the chair away from me! Now standing, I had my ration book taken and was asked some questions then dismissed. It was a strange start.

The next day we started receiving our innoculations in preparation for travel. We also had to sign a declaration to say that we would abide by the 'Rules and Regulations' of the Army. We were given cursory training in drill and how and who to salute, fitted for our uniforms and that was that. We were in the Army!

My first run-in with this new set of rules was close by and involved the afore-mentioned dress uniforms. We received all our 'khakis' from the Quartermaster but our dress uniforms were commissioned from Moss Bros. in London. The measurements were sent up and the uniforms received back. However there must have been a few amendments needed to the new dress uniforms and some were returned for alteration. When they were ready someone was needed to fetch them back. Most of the other girls were quite poorly that day from their typhoid inoculation. I was unaffected because I'd already been inoculated during my time at Croydon Mayday Hospital. So I was packed off on the train to London to collect the remaining uniforms. I thought I'd make a day of it and arranged to meet up with a friend who worked up in London. We went for some lunch and had a great time. I collected the uniforms and returned to Barracks by around 6pm. To my surprise I was called in for a telling-off. It was then that the full realisation that I was no longer a free agent dawned on me and I thought to myself, 'Be careful here – this is the Army now!' I quickly concocted a story about how I'd arrived at Waterloo and started to feel ill from the typhoid jab … They let me off that time and I learned a valuable lesson for the future.

4

Nursing for the Army

My first posting was to Colchester. They had a very large hospital there but I was a bit disappointed to find my job was on the Surgical Ward and not in Theatre as I had requested. During my initial interview with the Army I was told there was a shortage of Theatre Sisters and that there would be no problem posting me in this role.

As part of the handover from the Sister who was leaving, the Quartermaster took an inventory of all the equipment on the ward, which I then had to sign. From that point forward, anything missing from that inventory was my responsibility.

At Colchester the military hospital was run very differently from the hospitals I had worked at as a civilian. Everything looked very regimented. All the beds and lockers were aligned with millimetre precision. All the patients were in matching blue pyjamas and all the 'up-patients' (those well enough to help out with ward duties) wore blue jacket and trousers.

The up-patients would work around the ward and one of their main duties was to prepare the wards for inspection. For this they would straighten the beds and align them using lengths of string to make sure they were exactly positioned. This was done every day for the CO and the Matron's inspection!

After a while, when I felt I had found my feet I went to Matron to complain about my posting. I explained to her that I had wanted to work in the operating theatre. She informed me that to work in a military operating theatre I needed to pass Theatre Certification 1 and 2. Then I would be a qualified Theatre Sister.

An opportunity soon arose. One weekend when the main Theatre Sister at Colchester was on leave and the secondary Theatre Sister was ill, I was asked to stand in. At weekends, only emergency operations were undertaken. That weekend three ladies were admitted for emergency operations. The procedures in the operating theatre were very different from those I had experienced in civilian life. I suggested some improvements that revealed to the chief surgeon that I was already an experienced Theatre Sister and he was impressed enough to award me the Theatre Certification 1.

It soon transpired that a Theatre Sister was needed at the hospital in Bovington Tank Depot, Dorset and I was posted there. Unfortunately, there were very few operations performed here and so I was finding it very difficult to get my Theatre Certificate 2. The Army surgeon was actually based at Chester and only came down for emergencies. I was there six months before I complained and was sent to the Cambridge Military Hospital at Aldershot to get the experience I needed to gain my second certificate. It was immediately apparent that the existing Theatre Sister there and I did not get along. In an attempt to make life difficult for me, Sister assigned me to assist the civilian surgeon, who came each week to conduct operations at the hospital. He had a reputation as being a bit quick, very efficient and expecting the same from his staff and could therefore be rather tricky to work with. On my first week there, Sister asked me to assist him in theatre, only telling me his name was Mr Wright. This was a familiar name to me and I was certain from his reputation that this was the same surgeon I had worked with at RSC Guildford. I had worked with him on many operations and knew his ways and prepared the instruments and trolley in exactly the way I knew would assist him the most. When he arrived, everything was ready, and I was fully gowned up for the operations. He didn't recognise me and we worked through four operations speaking very little. At the end of the session I spoke to him and said 'You were a bit slow today?' and pulled off my mask. Needless to say he was very surprised to see me and he swore at me but we both had a good laugh! Not long after this incident I was assisting the Head of Surgery at the Cambridge with a burst peptic ulcer, something I'd had experience with before, and he was so impressed with me that he immediately awarded me my Theatre Certificate 2. I was only at The Cambridge for one week before returning to Bovington as a fully qualified Theatre Sister.

I really enjoyed my time at Bovington and there were a few funny events worth recounting. For instance, the Quartermaster (QM) would have random stock checks of all the equipment assigned to the ward e.g. brushes, brooms and so on. If there was anything found missing it was the rule that whoever was responsible for that piece of equipment would pay for a replacement. Once an 'Axes, chopping' was found missing and I was down as the person responsible for it. (The axe was required on the ward to chop firewood for the fires that heated the ward.) What I found out was that everyone (except the QM) on the ward had known for some time that the axe was missing and had used various ways to cover it up. I was not prepared to get involved in this charade and wanted a fresh start and so I came clean to the QM about the axe. Fortunately for me the QM was happy to write it off and start again.

Another funny thing happened. As the Bovington hospital was an old hutted hospital it was rotting in places. One day I heard an almighty crash in Matron's office (just next to Theatre). The surgeon and I were just having coffee and we went to see what had happened. We opened the door to Matron's office to find her practically lying on the floor with her feet up on the desk above her. The floorboards beneath her chair had rotted through and her chair had crashed through the boards leaving her in a rather undignified position. Thankfully she was alright. We all laughed about it later!

It was at Bovington Camp that I learnt to drive a three-ton lorry. There were two of us girls and six men and we had to go to the Tank Depot and learn about the gears etc. We girls giggled a bit – the men were very serious but we all learned to drive the three-ton truck. I loved it because it was so big and the driving seat so high up I could see all around me and passed my HGV test first time in Bournemouth. I enjoyed driving the lorry and had more confidence in it than driving an ordinary motor car, even though I learned to drive a car and got my international driving licence in Malta.

Many years later I returned to Bovington between overseas postings and was happy to see that the old hospital had been updated.

This second time, I was still a Theatre Sister but, like everyone else, was expected to take my turn on night duty. On a tour of night duty one looked after all the wards. It was during one of these tours that I had a very odd experience. A soldier's wife was in having her baby, which I delivered without mishap. The main ward was full and so I put her into a side room after her baby girl was delivered. That night I kept a close eye on her and they both seemed comfortable. In those days husbands visited at night and on the second night of that tour her husband approached me to ask if his wife could be moved from the side room. I answered that she could as there was now room on the main ward but enquired why. He informed me that his wife had seen a man all dressed in white standing in the corner of the room the night before and didn't want to spend another night there. At that point I remembered that I had heard that Lawrence of Arabia, who had lived his last years nearby, had died in that room following a motorbike accident. I asked him if either of them had heard the story about Lawrence of Arabia but it was clear they hadn't so I did not pursue that line of enquiry any further. I must say that although I went into that room several times at night, I never actually saw anything myself but it has always left me wondering …

5

Nursing Overseas

Egypt

My first posting overseas was to Egypt in the Canal Zone. The ship that took us to Egypt had previously been one of King Farouk's personal yachts, the *El Nil*. It had been confiscated and converted into a hospital ship. Although small, she was lovely. The ship would drop me in Egypt around November en route to Singapore where she would drop off six other nurses and some troops. Unfortunately, the ship had been badly neglected and as we entered the Bay of Biscay the ship suffered engine failure. She started to move in circles and made us all very seasick. We docked at Malta for repairs and after about two days there we continued on to Port Said. Once again crossing the Mediterranean, we had engine trouble but eventually we reached Port Said. The ship had been well stocked with food and alcohol for the trip to Singapore near Christmas time but by the time we reached Port Said all the alcohol was gone. We'd had quite a good time on the journey!

After dropping me off at Port Said the *El Nil* continued on its way to Singapore. She had trouble again and had to dock in Mombasa. She was inspected there and taken out of service as it was deemed unsafe. This is why we'd had such a rough journey. My first sea trip had been a bit of a 'baptism of fire'. Thankfully I have never been seasick since. In fact my first trip to a foreign country was also quite the baptism of fire. Back then in Egypt everyone was wearing robes like pyjamas, everything was very different from England.

I joined the troop train at Port Said to Fayid. I found it very interesting going through the villages. The hospital was by the Great Bitter Lake in the desert. It was a 300 bed hutted hospital. My first morning in Fayid was interesting. I was very tired and when it was morning I awoke to find a man (a Zafragi, Egyptian for workman) standing in front of me. I was very startled and let out a shout but all he wanted was to know if I took sugar in my tea! It was a shock to the system to find that the toilets were not pull chains but buckets. The emptying of these was very well organised. Three times a day an open lorry arrived with bins covered with sacking saturated with disinfectant. The arrival came with a lot of noise, a lot of smells and many flies! One poor Sister, new to the hospital, got 'gyppy' tummy and was giving her all into a bucket, when the trapdoor opened and a cheerful Egyptian voice said, 'One moment, Sit (Madam)' and then the bucket was removed, cleaned, disinfected and returned. I am proud to say, that unlike nursing in our hospitals today, we had very little cross infection. This was due to army discipline and nursing of a very high standard. In one period we admitted thirty cases from the RAF with typhoid. No other patient and no staff were infected and all thirty recovered except one.

I think the Army should be very proud of the BMH Fayid – I know I was.

On our nights off we would go into Cairo and stay at the Carlton Hotel. Once my friend and I had our breakfast up in the room when there was a knock on the door. I answered it to a man with a bunch of flowers. He asked for 'Sutton' and when I asked him what he wanted, he tried to give me the flowers but I told him I didn't want them. He insisted and informed me that they were sent by a man who was waiting downstairs to see me. I was bemused as I didn't know anyone in Cairo. When I went down to the lobby a man approached me and introduced himself as 'Mammoud's father'.

Mammoud was an attendant at our staff dining room back in Fayid. I had befriended him and he had asked me to take a letter to the reception desk at the Carlton Hotel on my visit there. I didn't really know what Mammoud's father wanted, but he offered to be our guide around Cairo for our stay. I explained that I didn't have the money to pay him but he insisted that he would be offended if we tried to pay him. He explained that he was the official guide at the hotel and that his son had asked him to look after us while we were in Cairo.

He showed us around in a taxi and I explained to him again that we didn't have much money so there was no point taking us to expensive places. He took us to the 'Musci' which was like a very narrow lane full of souk-like shops. At one shop they offered us coffee and water so I explained to them that I was sorry but I didn't have any money to spend in their shop. They didn't seem to mind and told us to enjoy looking around.

The owner came up to me and I explained our pecuniary situation to him also, but he insisted that we just enjoy looking around his shop. The shop was fabulous with all sorts of treasures, fabrics and perfumes. There was a ring that caught my eye that I kept going back to. It fascinated me. It was a scarab ring. The owner explained that it was an authentic ring from a pharaoh's tomb and I could have that verified by the museum. He said I could have it and if I gave him a cheque for £12 (a lot of money in 1949) and if I then decided that I did not want it he would return the cheque to me. I still have the ring today.

On the second day Mammoud's father, Sayid, took us to the pyramids at Giza which in those days was far from the city in the desert. It was magical and beautiful back then. Unfortunately, visitors today will find the city has expanded to swallow up and tower over the pyramids.

Mammoud turned out to be a good friend indeed. Once back at the hospital my big toe became infected. I had to wait for my night off to have it operated on to remove the nail. After the op they dumped me back in my room and I was pretty much left to fend for myself. Hours passed and no one came to see if I was alright or needed food or even a drink. I'd missed the dining room and the staff in charge of menus hadn't checked if I wanted anything. I was hot, tired and thirsty but I couldn't walk on my foot as it was very painful. I just suffered in silence. I was feeling pretty sorry for myself when I heard a tap at the door. I called 'come in' and there was Mammoud. He'd noticed that I hadn't been to the dining hall for dinner and wondered what had happened to me. I showed him my foot and he understood. He went off to the kitchen and came back with some food and squash and I was so grateful to him. He could have lost his job if anyone had found out he'd been to my quarters.

I was off on sick leave for three days before I had to go back to work. My foot was still very sore and when I turned up on the Minor Septic Ward there were at least four other soldier patients in for the same thing as I had. They were being better cared for though, but not for long as I soon got them out of bed and walking!

When in Egypt I had a great social life. At one point I had two boyfriends simultaneously. This was a bit difficult at times. I was pretty serious about one of the chaps but I had suspicions that he was married, so I kept him at arm's length. When I was subsequently posted back home I didn't hear from him again. However, ten years later he simply turned up at the mess of the station I was posted to and asked to see me. The first thing I said to him was 'How's your wife?' He seemed surprised and replied 'How did you know I was married, I have only been married for two years now?' He explained that he had only married her because she looked like me. I was shocked. I think I would have married him back then if he had asked me. We went out to lunch for old times sake and that was the end of that, or so I thought. Many years later he contacted me again and by this time I was living in my current home in Godalming. I had the house to myself that weekend so I invited him to stay. We got to talking about old times and he asked me, 'If I had asked you to marry me back in Egypt would you?' I said, 'Definitely yes,' and he said 'What a mess!' He was still married at that point but spending time with him that weekend, I came away with the feeling that actually I had had a lucky escape and I realised I no longer had any feelings for him.

Malta

Overseas postings were for a maximum of three years and after two years at Fayid I was posted to Malta. After Fayid, the hospital at Malta was well equipped and well built. Shortly after I arrived, two aircraft carriers docked in Grand Harbour each with cases of a different strain of polio. One was called *The Ocean*, a British vessel and the other *The Magnificent*, a Canadian vessel. We had an isolation ward in which there were four iron lungs. The men were admitted and four patients had to be treated in the machines. The electricity supply in Malta at the time was quite erratic, so we had to have a squad of ORs (Other Ranks) on permanent standby to crank the generators by hand. In time, with a lot of intensive nursing, all the men recovered although some with permanent disability. We were very proud of this and also very proud of the fact that no other patient or member of staff contracted the infection. This was purely down to high standards of cleanliness and discipline in the hospital.

Except for those in the iron lungs all the Canadians and British were in the same ward and this worked quite well. Although they were very weak and poorly they entertained each other. However, there was one patient, a Canadian, who regularly upset the general harmony of the ward. He was quite a small man (I don't know if this was significant) but he was rude and arrogant to everyone without exception. The Canadians took it upon themselves to sort him out. On one occasion, I heard an almighty commotion and I thought to myself 'they must be getting better.' I went to see what was happening. About four chaps had grabbed the little guy and manhandled him into a bath of cold water. Unfortunately this did not improve his general demeanour one bit! Another time, in preparation for some VIP visitors, I arranged for them to cut each other's hair. The locals were terrified at the mention of the word polio. They had had some bad breakouts of the disease in their own community and would not come near us even after the quarantine period was over. Anyway to get their own back on 'Mr Rude' they pinned him down and gave him a Mohican! It was cause for some amusement amongst the visitors and it did seem to quieten him down for a while.

We had a fantastic social life while stationed at Malta. Grand Harbour was always full of ships from the Royal Navy and we were often invited aboard for film shows and dancing. We had to have plenty of evening dresses (mufti as we called it). Dress uniform was only used on very special formal occasions. In a shop in Valletta I bought a black strapless evening dress with a very fitted bodice and a taffeta skirt covered in lace and though I say so myself, I looked stunning in it. The owner of the shop was so impressed she asked me if I would model for her, but I had to decline as the Army would not allow it. However I did get many partners whenever I was wearing the dress!

One of the things I liked to do while in Malta in my free time was to go to musical performances, opera and so on. One particular occasion, Maria Callas visited Malta with Tito

Gobbi and gave three performances in one of the large halls in Valetta (there was no theatre there at that time). At this stage in her life she was quite plump and in my humble opinion her voice was better than when she was slimmer. This occasion stands out in my mind as I enjoyed it so much.

We always held cocktail parties on Corps Days. All the dignitaries would be invited and once this included Lady Mountbatten of Burma. At the time her husband, Lord Mountbatten, was Governor of Malta and she liked to visit us regularly. I had met her at the hospital several times and I had found her to be a charming woman. She got to know all the nursing officers by name. She arrived at our cocktail party on time, but without her husband, who arrived later. When he eventually arrived, Matron asked me to get him a drink. Being a cocktail party he asked, 'What muck have you got?' A little put out by this, I informed him that he would be offered our special cocktail. He accepted it and asked me what was in it, so I told him, 'I can't tell you – it's a secret.' So I got my own back in a way!

I was nearly at the end of my short service commission (five years) and Lady Mountbatten asked me, 'You're not leaving?' I explained that I would like to become a Regular but for that I needed recommendations through my Confidential Reports and she gave me a knowing look and said, 'I'm sure that won't be a problem.' Lo and behold, I became a Regular, maybe it was a coincidence, but I don't think so.

Whilst in Malta I had occasion to bump into Prince Philip three times. The first time I was at a Red Cross fundraiser concert. When my friend and I arrived we found our pre-booked seats and sat down. They were one row back from the front. Shortly after we sat down, the lights went out for the performance to begin. I noticed that there were four empty seats in front of us and thought 'Oh good.' Just then, four

Royal Naval officers arrived to take up the seats in front of us. Although I myself am tall, the chap who sat in front of me was now badly blocking my view. I muttered, just loud enough for him to hear, 'Can't see a bloody thing now!' The chap then turned around and said, 'sorry old girl,' and scooted down his seat. I recognised him as Prince Philip. 'Whoops!' I thought to myself.

The second time I bumped into him was at the Gunners' Ball in Valetta. We knew Prince Philip was to be there and we were under orders to wear white gloves in case we were presented to him at any point. Late on in the evening the word went round that he had left, so we all relaxed and set about enjoying ourselves. We all got a bit tight, the lights were turned down low and it was all very romantic. I was dancing with my boyfriend, when we sort of crashed into another dancing couple and ended up with each others dancing partner. I found myself dancing with Prince Philip! Diplomatic to the core, I exclaimed 'Oh my God!' Fortunately, my partner had the wit to rescue me before I said any more. He apologised to Prince Philip for the stumble but he was actually fine about it and we all had a laugh. Between you and me I think he was a bit tight too!

The third time was while I was at a Maltese friend's house in Gozo. Carmelina's brother was the Chief Medical Officer for Health for Gozo and it was actually his house we were visiting for a few days. On the day we arrived on Gozo we found out that Prince Philip and Princess Elizabeth were on a State Visit to the island. As we travelled round the island to see the sights we kept running into the Royal Cavalcade. Our driver tried some back roads to try to avoid them and get us home. Unfortunately, the Royal party must have had the same idea and we turned a corner and ploughed straight into them, knocking a motorcycle outrider off his bike. There was Prince Philip glaring at me. I shrunk into the car seat. He probably thought, 'It's that woman again!'

While in Malta I kept in touch with a QA friend I left behind in Egypt. She was now in Suez, but during some leave she decided to visit me in Malta. We were both excited to be seeing each other and having good times. As she was arriving by troop ship she joked that she wanted to arrive to a twenty-one gun salute with the band playing. As it happened there was a Naval exercise that included US, UK and Canadian ships taking place in the Mediterranean. At the end of the exercise several of the ships with the most senior officers on board were to be docked in Grand Harbour. For their arrival, there would be a gun salute and a band. They all arrived at the same time as Doreen and so she got her twenty-one gun salute and the band played!

6

Neurosurgery training

After three years abroad (Egypt then Malta) I was posted home. One of my boyfriends from Egypt was still overseas but was due back in the UK after his three-year stint in a few months time. He was keen for me to stay in the UK so that we could hook up again. The only way that I could do this easily was to do a course. I asked to do the 'Neurosurgery for Theatre Sisters Course' with the neurosurgeon. He was a civilian employed by the government for all neurosurgical operations required for the Royal Navy and the British Army. He was well known in nursing circles as being excellent with his patients but very difficult to work with. We nicknamed him 'God'. Mostly, one did not ask to go on his course, one was sent. However, it was convenient for me and, when I was accepted, I found myself posted to Wheatley near Oxford for at least the next year (six months course plus six months experience while training the next sister).

I knew the outgoing Theatre Sister already and she had warned me how dreadful 'God' could be. He often upset her to the point that her tears threatened to contaminate the theatre equipment. She introduced me to 'God'. He was quite short compared to me and from the outset he irritated me by calling me 'nurse' knowing full well I was a Sister. One day we were all in theatre – 'God', the current Theatre Sister and myself. This was about the sixth case I had attended as an observer and 'God' was just getting into his stride, abusing and insulting the Theatre Sister. Although this was a regular occurrence, she had clearly reached her limit; she was very stressed and just fainted onto the theatre floor. I tried to catch her but it was too late. With the help of some orderlies

I carried her out of theatre and brought her round. However, she became hysterical so I telephoned Matron. I explained to her what had happened. She said, 'That dreadful little man! I'll arrange for Sister to be brought over to the Mess.' I went back into theatre and asked 'God' if he wanted me to scrub up. He replied, 'Please yourself,' so I said, 'Well then, I won't,' and quite irritated he said, 'Oh I'm fed up with you women and your monthlies'. I was very cross and told him 'If you think Sister was menstruating you are mistaken! It was you who made her faint and now she refuses to come back to Theatre ever again.' Later the Colonel-in-Charge of Theatre (who was also the Anaesthetist) asked me if I would take over as Theatre Sister. I said I would but I warned him that I wouldn't be leaving theatre in tears or having hysterics and in fact I'd be more likely to lose my temper if 'God' got up to his tricks with me.

After about three cases, during which 'God' had been fairly tolerable, he started to abuse me in a similar way to the previous Sisters. Firstly, when I placed the correct instrument directly into his hand he started throwing them back at me. He caught me with a scalpel and cut my finger. It was bleeding and so I had to change my gloves. Next he threw a bone nibbler at me and cut my thumb and I had to change my gloves again. He shouted at me, 'How can I operate with a fool like you around?' – his usual routine. By this time I'd had just about as much as I was going to take from him and I completely lost my temper. I grabbed the nearest thing to me which happened to be an artery forcep and was about to throw it at him whilst swearing when the Colonel-in-charge screamed 'No!' I stopped short of throwing it directly at 'God' and it landed on the floor. I then had one of the staff take it out of theatre and have it sterilised. Meanwhile, 'God', rather taken aback at my outburst asked if I now felt better. I replied 'No I do not!' and he looked around the theatre and said, 'We've got a right one here.' I then told him, 'If you want any more instruments take them from the table yourself, as I'll hand you no more.' After the operation was finished the Warrant Officer, a very nice man, told me that he would take the patient off the table and that he had left me a cup of tea in my office. Relieved it was all over, I thanked him and went to get my tea. I found 'God' in my office sitting at my desk looking as if he was about to drink my tea. Still fuming from before I said, 'Abuse me at the Theatre you might, but drink my tea you won't!' and I lifted my tea and walked out of the room.

I thought that this must be the end of my career in the Army. There was no way they would let me get away with this. However, I never heard another thing about it and the next day I scrubbed up as normal. After the incident life progressed fairly tolerably and if ever 'God' started getting carried away again I would immediately stop putting the instruments into his hand and start putting them onto his table as a little reminder.

When my year was up and I had trained up the incoming Theatre Sister, ready to take over from me, 'God' informed me that he had spoken with the Ministry of Defence and I was to stay until he said I could go. He kept me there for three years in total.

Finally the three years was up and even 'God' couldn't keep me any longer. At what I considered to be my final operation I let this be known to 'God'. At the time he just said 'Hmph' but after the op he came strolling into my office and said 'What do you mean you're leaving? Why don't you come and be my Theatre Sister at my civilian hospital?' But I said 'No' and to my surprise he kissed me and told me that if ever I needed a job or was in trouble or needed help anywhere in the world I was to call him. Then he hugged me and that was that.

Despite the initial rough ride I did have good times at Wheatley and made some lifelong friends there. In fact, during my time at Wheatley, there were two young National Servicemen working in the Theatre as orderlies. I remember that, although they led me a bit of a dance, they were exceptionally good at their jobs. Many years later, after they had been trying to find me to thank me for their start in nursing, I was delighted to receive a telephone call from one of them. He said, 'Thank goodness we have found you.' Since then they have been to visit me and one of them is now a grandfather.

After Wheatley I was sent overseas again and while stationed in Sierra Leone I did have occasion to deal with 'God' one more time. A VIP collapsed at a function at the base out there and I was called in to nurse him. It was decided to contact 'God' and inform him of the man's condition. He received the message while operating at Wheatley. The Sister there, who was a friend of mine, wrote to me later to tell me what had happened. Apparently 'God' was heard to say, 'That woman Sutton is there. Ask her if I should come.' I was indeed asked, but this was not normal procedure and as such caused the authorities and me much embarrassment. My response at the time was 'If you have to operate we haven't got the instruments we need, so you will have to bring them.' He then replied, 'Well, I shan't come then,' and so a neurologist was sent instead. I am pleased to say the patient survived and when he was well enough he was returned to the UK by ship with a medical officer in attendance. His wife wrote to me to say that he eventually made a complete recovery. I had asked the patient to tell 'God' that he was my special patient and he was to look after him well. I heard via the grapevine that 'God's' response to this was, 'If that woman said so then I must do it!'

I was very sad to find that having been a professor, 'God' died of a cerebral accident. In spite of my initial opinion of him, I did, in time, come to respect and admire him.

7

Two years in Sierra Leone

We left Blackbushe by air and after many stops arrived at the airport near Freetown, which was miles away from the town itself in a bush clearing with very few facilities. When leaving the aircraft I was horrified by the heat.

To go to Freetown by road was nearly one hundred miles. The quickest way was by boat over the bay, which took about half an hour. Transport was waiting for me and I was taken up to Wilberforce (the hospital). My posting was for two years and I arrived one year before Sierra Leone got its independence, but I stayed on for another year. I thought the coming of independence would give them much pleasure, only to find a lot of the staff unhappy. They said, 'who will look after us when you have gone?' I was surprised that the same thing happened in Kenya when they got their Yuhuru independence.

The hospital and our quarters were on a hill. Being high up it was cooler and the view beautiful. My quarters were very comfortable but like all buildings had a tin roof. I was introduced to my houseboy whose name was Momo. He spoke Pidgin English, which took me some time to understand and speak. He was a little man and to my horror had filed teeth so they were pointed, which indicated that he came from a cannibal tribe. I found that I was the owner of a cat in residence from the previous occupant. My appointment was as a theatre sister and I was also in charge of the ward for African other ranks. Although a small hospital it dealt with every type of medical need. It was built on stilts, because of the insect and animal life beneath. One ward we couldn't use because the boards had been so eaten away by woodworm. It left us with a maternity ward, one for warrant officers' wives and children and two other wards, one for warrant officers and the other for officers. In another block was an African ward and adjacent to it was the theatre and an outpatients department for the soldiers only. Another department in a separate block was for the outpatients of the wives and children of the other ranks.

It was quite a shock when meal times came round. The food came from the African cookhouse in large buckets, some with rice and some with a sort of stew of either fish or meat, neither of which had been boned. It smelt very nice, but I found that all my patients took their food from the plate with their fingers and spat out all the bones round their beds which were swept up with palm fronds. Brushes were supplied but my staff, all being African, much preferred the palm, which they used in their homes.

In the rainy season, known as the Rain Palaver when it rained almost continually, laundry was a problem. It all came back damp. In the dry season, known as Dry Palaver, it came back beautifully ironed, but I doubt if it was washed properly there being a shortage of water.

Because of the climate, we only worked half-day mornings and half-day afternoons. One sister would be delegated for night coverage and so would be on call. Though one had to have leave, there was nowhere to go. Being the only theatre sister I was always on call and so when off duty had to notify people where I was going. Most of the time I went down to the beach and if needed, a jeep arrived with a flag flying. Most people knew me and would call 'Rosemary, you are wanted!'

I found working in the operating theatre a bit alarming until I got used to it. There were no windows in any of the hospital areas, only fly and thief wire and wooden shutters. It was a common occurrence when operating to find you had an audience looking through the wire, who had to be chased away.

All my orderlies were African and they refused to wear white boots in the theatre, so I had to fill a container with mild disinfectant and my staff had to put their feet in before going into theatre proper. In charge of my staff was an African, Sgt. Williams, who was very efficient and was also in charge of the male outpatients department. He normally gave the injections after I had checked them, but when he was away a L/Cpl. was in charge. I told him to get everything ready and I would come and give the injections, only to arrive and be confronted with ten bare African bottoms!

Sgt. Williams went up country to his small coffee plantation. He asked for leave to go and brush the coffee. When he was away his mother was in charge, but she was a leper and we used to send treatment for her from the hospital, for which she was very grateful and always sent me back a dash, which means a gift. I got rotten eggs, fruit and on one occasion I was told she had sent me back a live dash, which I found in my office cupboard and it was a tortoise!

Sgt. Williams told me about his wives and life. He had several young men visiting when he was on duty, whom he introduced to me as his sons. They were all by different mothers. He then told me that he had one Christian wife, four tribal wives and four concubines, who were rotated according to their condition. This meant that he had his Christian wife living with him in married quarters, but she couldn't reproduce, much to his sorrow. We found on examining her that she had an ovarian cyst, which we removed and she became pregnant and had a daughter who was christened and named after me, Rosemary. His many wives and concubines went up to the plantation to help the mothers when they were pregnant. After they had given birth they returned to Freetown and another took their place.

Sgt. Williams said to me one day that he had asked all the previous Sisters if he could go to the Cambridge Military Hospital at Aldershot to do a course in the theatre there. On every occasion he was turned down because they said they could not manage without him. I spoke to the CO and said if they could arrange for him to go to the Cambridge I would manage for three months. And so he went, and even visited my father. After he came back I was able to give him much more responsibility and he was proud that his name and what he had done was in the local newspaper.

One corporal was admitted with a bad heart condition and we were very worried about him because he did not seem to be responding to treatment. Sadly, when I was in my office I heard some of the patients laughing and when I went out to see what was going on they pointed to this man and said, 'look, he done go die,' and sadly he had.

We weren't allowed to admit any of the African children but on one occasion after the morning outpatients had finished, a little boy was found by me and on investigation we discovered that his parents had left him and gone up country, so we had to admit him. He was of a tribe that nobody in the Freetown area could understand, and was very undernourished and quite ill. I tried to make him drink and eat and he would not, but eventually I tempted him with a chocolate biscuit, which he loved. I then had to introduce him to a more suitable diet, which I finally managed and he improved. The trouble was he was so attached to me that when he saw me about and I would not take with me, he cried and screamed so loudly that most of the time I was on duty he sat on my hip and wouldn't let go. So people got used to seeing sister with a pickin! Eventually one of the African warrant officers took charge of the boy and he was seen with a pickin on his hip! Later the child's parents came back to Freetown and he was reunited with them. About three months later when I was passing Outpatients Department all hell was let loose because the child had seen me and wanted to come after me. So again I had to have him on my hip and give him chocolate biscuits before he would go back to his parents.

I soon learned about palaver. You would have a genuine patient admitted to the hospital with back pain or a serious eye condition called river blindness. Others soon realised that this was a good way out of any special event they wanted to avoid and also when it was the rainy season. The civilians would commit some sort of offence and be put in jail because they would be warm, dry and fed. The soldiers thought that the hospital was the place to be admitted. So we had the back and the eye palaver, where you would find the patient being helped up to the hospital by his friend, limping very badly as if it was his back hurting him, and another one being led by the hand saying that he could not see. One had to admit them in case it was a serious condition. I soon had my suspicions about this and found a way to test them. When I went on duty I would go to each patient on the ward and ask how the body was and would find out the condition of the patient. While passing the bed of the patient with the 'bad' back or 'eye condition' and a couple of beds beyond, I would take out my handkerchief to blow my nose and drop paper money. When I looked round to the suspicious patients they were usually out of bed picking it up. Knowing this would happen I would turn round sharply and exclaim, 'It's a miracle – you are better!' and the man was discharged, much to the delight of the patients who knew that this Madame knew all about this palaver.

At night the ward was sealed by the shutters and the doors were locked. So it was very difficult to get in if you were worried about any patient. So unless we were very worried we needn't bother as they had a telephone and could ring for help. This particular night I had to go to the theatre to arrange for a Caesarean section operation. I had been worried about one of the patients in the ward and decided I would try to get in to see how he was. I banged on the door and the shutters and got no answer. So I thought I would ring on the phone and see what was going on but no one answered the phone. We did the operation, which was a success, and in the morning I went down to the ward, which was now open, went in and said to the Night Orderly 'How's the body?' They were all looking very scared. 'Madame, we no sleep all night – the juju man tried to get in and he even tried to get in through the telephone, but we no answered.'

Thieving was a way of life. The first Christmas I was there in my quarter, it was dark and I heard some little pickin singing *Away in a manger*. I opened the door and was confronted with six little boys all about six-years-old and another one about ten. I was so moved that I gave them a big dash (money). About a fortnight later I was burgled by the tief men. The older boy, having seen what was worth taking in my shamba through the open door, told his parents, who decided to come and get what they could find, which they did.

There are snakes galore in Africa – saw them every day. Frogs were numerous and at night, until I got used to it, I found it difficult to sleep for their croaking. My quarters, having a tin roof, would also become very noisy at times as there was a very large tree overhanging the roof which periodically produced fruit with stones and the fruit bat came at night and spat out the pips. Fruit bats I found were lovely and often slept in the daytime on the same tree. Butterflies and moths were huge and beautiful and there was a variety of birds. There were six African grey parrots that lived in the area and were terribly noisy.

The African juju was to me a nonsense, and the witchdoctors a joke. I soon changed my opinion when a young recruit was admitted very ill. Although we tried we couldn't diagnose his condition. One of his friends who came to visit him said that because he had joined the army against his tribe's wishes, the witchdoctor had put a juju on him and he would die. In spite of all our efforts to save him, he died.

Juju has its funny side. The Matron of the hospital didn't get on very well with the African staff. One of the waiters in the Mess was rude to her and she sacked him on the spot. He said he wouldn't go until he got his money, though he knew she couldn't pay him and he had to go through the Admin Officer. It was a Saturday and he couldn't be paid until the Monday. Having an audience by this time, he struck her in the face and knocked her glasses off, and wouldn't let her go to her own quarters. So she phoned me at the hospital and said 'Come at once.' I got into my car and drove down to the Mess. I was known as 'Na Big One'! I got out of the car and took her into her quarters. I sent for the police and the doctor and went back on duty. The Matron was very worried about her safety and a guard was put on her quarters, but this didn't last for very long. So the night watchman was told he must sit by her apartment, which he did. Matron found it very difficult to sleep and began to look ill, so I gave her a sleeping tablet and told her that as I had a day off next day, I wouldn't go to sleep until light in the morning. Having no glass in the window I listened outside her window and she was obviously asleep. So I went to my quarters, washed my hair, put it in rollers, creamed my face and having no radio to listen to, I wrote some letters, read a book and eventually turned my light out at about three in the morning. I was just getting comfortable in bed, when I heard a noise coming from her quarters, so I decided to investigate. On my way to her quarters, I picked up a brick which was lying in the road. As I stood under the mango tree to listen, a car came

Rosemary Sutton

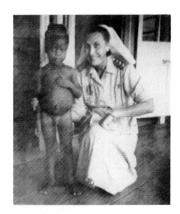

Left: Florence & Edward Sutton, parents of Rosemary
Above: Pickin on hip in Freetown, Sierra Leone

Left: Rosemary with the guide (our batman's father) in Egypt.
Above: Rosemary with Sgt. Williams, her senior orderly, outside the theatre in Freetown, Sierra Leone

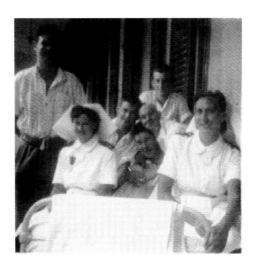

Patients with polio convalescing in Malta

Passing Out parade ~ early 1950s.
Rosemary first on left

Flamingos on Lake Nukuru

BMH Nairobi

D

Rosemary Sutton with sign at the
the North Frontier District

E

BMH Berlin

Rosemary Sutton at the Equator, Uganda

Elephants on the road to Mombasa, Kenya

Lions in Kenya

G

Rosemary Sutton on safari in Uganda

At Lake Victoria with SS Ugosa in the distance

H

by and I was silhouetted by car lights. There was a yell from the Matron's quarters and crashing in the bushes, but when I listened she was still asleep. I didn't see the night watchman but I assumed he had gone to investigate. I went back to my quarters and went to sleep.

At lunch the next day I asked Matron had she slept and she said 'Yes' – she felt much better. But we had a problem. The night watchman had resigned. He saw a powerful juju under the mango tree and had gone home to his family. Realising what had happened I decided to go and visit him. I said 'Pa, send your family away. I want to talk to you. Tell me about this juju.' He said it was big and shining and blue with horns. So I had to explain to him that African women had lovely curly hair, but lots of white women have straight hair and put rollers in to make it curly, and because of the sun white women put a lot of grease on their face. I also explained away the blue nightdress. I told him what to do. To go down to Freetown and tell all his friends there that there be a powerful juju in the Sisters' Mess Compound and he was the only person who could control it. This was to be a secret between us both. He came back and no one ever came to the Sisters' Mess Compound again. So he could sit on the verandah and sleep all night.

Momo, my houseboy, came to see me one afternoon when I was on duty to dress his eye and he told me that he had found a spitting cobra in the bathroom. When he went to kill it, it spat in his eye. The cobra escaped into the monsoon drain. I was not too happy having a bath for a few days but it did not return. Momo's eye was better after about a week.

Momo went to the NAAFI for some tinned cat food for my cat. When I pointed out how quickly the food was disappearing, Momo said it was too good for all of it to go to the cat so he took it for his pickin!

Rabies was prevalent in Sierra Leone, so one avoided being bitten by any animal. One of the officer's wives was bitten by a dog which was found to be rabid and she had to have many injections, but thankfully had no ill effects from the bite.

At a cocktail party, I was asked by the officer in charge of the battalion, who had to go up country to inspect a battalion, at a place called Bo, if I would like to go with him. I said I would love to, but I couldn't go as I was the only theatre sister and was always on call. He said, 'That's stupid – I'll speak to the Brigadier,' which he did, and the Brigadier said, 'Stupid – of course she can go.' So the next day I said to the Matron, 'I am going up country for the weekend with the Colonel' and she said 'You can't go.' I said, 'The Brigadier said I can,' and the CO, not wanting to upset anyone, decided that I could go, in which case any operations that were needed during the weekend would have to go to the Civilian Nursing Home, which was quite near the hospital. As luck would have it, three patients needed operations, but I don't know how much it cost the Army!

I thoroughly enjoyed my weekend away and had my own quarters and a houseboy. One afternoon the Colonel and I were invited to visit the compound of the Diamond Corporation. After going through the bush for about half an hour we came to a tarmacked road which went into a very large protected area. We had to go through a gate which was guarded by armed men, into a large compound with nice houses and gardens and a golf course and landing area for small airplanes. The wives were confined to the compound except when they wanted to return to South Africa. We had lunch with the manager from the Diamond Corporation and after lunch were asked if we would like to see some diamonds and we both said 'Yes'. So we left the compound and went out into the bush to another compound with armed guards and guard dogs. We were taken upstairs to a small office, which was open at the front, so that one could see what was going on in the rest of the building. On a platform, nearly at the roof of the building were Africans in loin cloths. They had very large sacks of soil which they tipped onto a platform, with water which then ran down to the ground on runners with a wire mesh dividing the soil from the stones and diamonds. At the bottom stood Africans with one arm encased in sacking, using the other hand to pick up the stones with forceps. The diamonds were then put into cigarette tins which were marked to show where the diamonds had come from. They were then sent to the Diamond Corporation in different parts of the world to be cut and polished.

I was invited to a cocktail party, where I first met John who was a diamond buyer for the Diamond Corporation. We got on quite well together. When he went back up country we used to correspond a lot. Phoning was difficult – you couldn't always get the person you wanted to speak to. Infrequently he could fly down to Freetown and take me out and tell me all his news.

One incident I remember, was one night he was woken up after a heavy drinking session by his houseboy, accompanied by a tribesman, who produced a large rough diamond from his mouth. John gave him ten pounds for it and he went away happy. The next night when he went to bed, John remembered the diamond which was on his bedside table. He realised that it was a big stone which he sent to the Diamond Corporation in London where they found it was of high value. When cut it was sold for many thousands of pounds.

Back on duty in the hospital one of my orderlies, a corporal, said his father was a paramount chief and in his shamba, the walls being made of mud, there were many rough diamonds. The corporal had quite a few in his pocket which he liked to rattle. There was in fact a law forbidding diamonds to be taken out of the country, except by the Diamond Corporation. This corporal was very arrogant and

I had much trouble with him. Having served lunch from the kitchen for the Europeans, who had beetroot in the salad, Doris, the ward maid, asked 'What was it?' I said, 'Would you like to taste it?' and she said, 'Yes' so I gave her some beetroot which made her lips red. The corporal then teased her and said, 'Like the white women.' He then went on to point out, as he saw it, the luxuries enjoyed by the white man – shoes, clothes, big houses etc. By this time I was getting angry, so I took him by the hand, opened the fridge door and put his hand in it. I then explained to him why the white man had shoes, clothes and brick houses etc., as they would freeze in the winter if they weren't so dressed. I explained to him that he never wore shoes because it was warm, he didn't need to have brick or wood houses which we had to pay for, because he could go into the bush and take whatever he wanted to make himself a shamba. And to eat, there was so much wild fruit that he could eat for nothing. This made him change his opinion somewhat and we got on better after that. It seems to me that the whole diamond business was unfair to the original finders of the stones. I can understand why diamonds are the cause of so much trouble in Sierra Leone.

The corporal in charge of the orderlies in the European Ward was known as Pa Willie – Pa being the equivalent of Mister. Pa Willie was marvellous with the children and they loved him. He used to take the temperature of the children and one little girl would not have her temperature taken by the Sister but would have Pa Willie. He explained to her, because she was very hot, that if she put the thermometer into her mouth and under her tongue all the hot would come out into the thermometer. He showed her how it had gone up and she believed him!

Doris, the ward maid had crinkly hair, a large nose, bust and bottom and flat feet. She was quite young, had a lovely disposition, and was always laughing. She was also an extremely hard worker. One morning one of the orderlies told me that Doris was sick. When I went to the kitchen to see her she looked so tired. I said 'What be the matter, Doris?' and she said, 'American ship in Kissi.' Fifteen men at 50 shillings each had made her very tired! So I did nothing more than send her home for the day. Some months later I was again called to the kitchen because Doris was sick. She looked dreadful. I thought of the Americans and said, 'Doris, you go catch pickin for belly.' She looked horrified and said, 'No Madame' and I said, 'How you know?' She said, 'I had my menses last week,' which meant she had menstruated, and really had got a stomach upset. Again I had to send her home.

Being a midwife myself and one of the team, we were all delighted when one of the officers' wives, over forty years old and with a poor history of pregnancy, came into labour and produced a 2lb 4oz baby girl. Despite no facilities for premature babies she survived and is now married with two sons of her own. I have been a friend of the family ever since.

The ward maid in the Maternity Department was a Creole called Princess. She was a beautiful girl and again a very hard worker. The warrant officer from Nigeria called Mr Ebomessi was in charge of the African staff employed in the hospital. He was a very efficient man who used to come to me if there was any trouble with my medical orderlies, and would ask me if he could put the individual on juju. This usually meant that he would have to do extra duties for two weeks. I usually said 'Yes'. He came to me one day and said 'What do you think of Princess?' I said I thought very highly of her and he said that he would like to marry her. But before he did, did I think she would be good for producing babies? He had honourable intentions but he wanted to be sure that Princess would give him a baby before he married her. I said that this was not our custom but I understood it was theirs and I thought she would be extremely suitable for him. So Princess had a baby and when she came back to work she brought the baby with her so I could see it. They married and when they got their independence, Mr Ebomessi was made a Captain and they had a European officer's quarters after he had returned to the UK. They had many children and were very happy. Sadly I don't know the outcome, because there was much fighting between the tribes and some of the officers who had been trained by the Europeans were killed.

The families in the barracks were brought to the Outpatients Department every morning by a very handsome African lady known as a Mammy Queen, who was in charge and kept good order. She was once sick herself with stomach pain so she had to undress for the doctor to examine her. Much to our horror her stomach was covered like a corset with telephone wire, which she was reluctant to take off. This was the cause of her stomach pain – she had obviously eaten too much and the stomach could not expand. She soon recovered and was sent home taking her telephone wire with her, so no doubt it went on again!

Many African women are very shrewd business women. One afternoon I had to go to the Post Office to collect a parcel and the Post Office closed at three o'clock so I had to run to get there before it closed. I was stopped in my tracks by an African lady with a parasol, who said, 'Stop – take my parasol. You are stupid in your white skin to run in this heat.' So I had to take her parasol to the Post Office, get my parcel and return to give her her parasol back. Is it any wonder that I have much affection for the Africans I met in Sierra Leone?

Most of the shopping was done in the cold store, which came in by boat twice a month from the UK, but some of the wives discovered that a butcher's shop had been opened in town with a very good butcher. He soon had a lot of custom from the wives, who were delighted to find fresh rather than frozen meat. Six months later, they were devastated to discover that the butcher had been arrested for cannibalism. So they were never sure what they had eaten. Thankfully we weren't worried in the Mess because we always got our meat from army rations and the cold store.

Some of the Africans realised what we had done for them and knew that when they came under their own Government they wouldn't be looked after quite so well.

One day, having time to spare before the bus left from Freetown up to Wilberforce, I went to an area called King Tom. I came across a little cemetery which was all overgrown and most of the gravestones were on the ground. But I managed to find one which was almost obliterated and the only thing that was clear was the QA badge. I was very moved to have found the resting place of a fellow QA in that unlikely spot, and said a little prayer.

Before we handed the hospital over we were visited by the Director of Medical Services. Panic set in to make sure that everything was up to inspection standard, and I am sorry to say that it wasn't. The day arrived for the inspection and the General, who was known to be very strict, was in a bad mood. He inspected the African ward and didn't get very much response from the patients, which irritated him. He went to go into a small side room, when I stopped him because I knew the floor was rotten. Also the African ward had only a bucket for toilet facilities, which had upset the General even more. The ward that had not been used, because of the floor being in such a bad condition, had got flush toilets but they were not attached to the sewage system, the pipes having been stolen, so whatever was flushed through the toilets simply went underneath the ward. The General, in spite of the rotten floor, demanded that the patients should be moved into the ward with the flush toilets. There were only a few places where one could put the beds safely. When I went on duty in the morning, I found all my patients had been moved to this ward and were very unhappy, but they were delighted with the toilet facilities and put everything possible through it! Having discovered an unpleasant odour emanating from the ward, I was very angry with the situation. The next day, while washing my hands in a bucket before going to lunch I saw the CO in the doorway and he said, 'What do you think of your new ward, Sister?' and I said, 'What idiot put my patients here – he should have his head examined.' The voice of the Inspecting Officer said, 'Would you have said that if you knew it was me!' and I said, 'Yes!' He said, 'Now they will have to renew parts of the floor,' and the wood was ordered and stacked.

About a week later, before I went to the Mess for my evening meal, I went down to the African ward. By this time it was dark. I realised that I had left my bag with my keys in it in the African ward and went to fetch it, only to find an empty ward and a lot of noise coming from the back of the ward. Looking out I saw all my patients with their pickin picking up the floorboards and putting them on their children's heads, who were going home with them. I thought this was very funny and went down to the Mess for my meal. In the morning when I went to do the round in the African ward I asked the usual greeting: 'How the body?' only to be told by the orderlies that they had had a terrible night because the tief man had been and taken all the timber. I said that they all be liars and that I came back last night and saw them putting timber on their pickins' heads to go to bush. They were all shattered by this. I am afraid I was on their side and laughed and said, 'But I no tell.' I know it was my duty to report it, but knowing their circumstances and how poor they were, I did not want to be the means of them being discharged from the Army.

As a white person I was liked by the Africans and to show their appreciation, the night before I left to go home they asked the CO if they could have a room to give me a party. The CO agreed. I was so overcome when I arrived and saw they had their wives with them, who had brought food to make a party. I was presented with a bottle of whisky, which they knew I liked, and a pair of slippers. As a matter of fact, I did shed a few tears but this was not the end of it. When I arrived on the ship there was a bit of a kerfuffle and I found that my cabin had been decorated with flowers and fruit. How they had managed to get the authority to do this was unheard of. When the ship sailed half my orderlies were on the dockside waving me off, and I cried.

Sgt. Williams, whom I mentioned earlier, would write to me and tell me how my god-daughter Rosemary was faring and give news of the hospital. Suddenly the letters stopped and though I wrote and asked why, I got no reply. Years later when I was working at the Cambridge Military Hospital in Aldershot, going to tea one afternoon in the Mess I found a large African lady sitting down talking to the rest of the members, and I was introduced. For some reason I did not like her. She said she was a trained nurse and was over to find out things about British Military Hospitals. I said, 'Where do you come from?' She said, 'Freetown.' I said, 'At Wilberforce?' She looked at me and I said, 'Before you got your independence I worked in that hospital.' I found out that she was living in my previous accommodation. I then asked what happened to WO2 Williams and she said, 'Don't speak to me about that man – we hung him!' It appeared that he had taken some of the instruments from the theatre and started his own little operating theatre, and unfortunately killed a man and buried him in the bush. So it goes to show however you think you know a man you don't really.

One afternoon, when giving a lecture, as usual half of my staff were asleep, so to wake them up I pointed to one and said, 'Why are you black and I am white?' At this remark all woke up and I said, 'When I came here what colour was I?' One said, 'White.' I said, 'And what colour am I now?' and they said, 'Na brown.' I asked, 'what caused this?' and they replied, 'The sun.' 'That is why God made you your colour, so that you don't burn like the white man does in the sun.' I then returned to the lecture and a wide-awake audience.

Having many happy memories of Freetown I went on a cruise which called in at Freetown, just to see how it was. We were met at the quayside by some ramshackle buses and a small female guide who gave us all little buttonholes of flowers. We got into the buses to have a tour and I asked her if the tour went to Wilberforce and she said, 'Yes'. I was horrified at the state of the roads and the buildings and the dirt. We went to Wilberforce – my little quarter was in ruins with no roof. What I could see of the barracks, although in use, was in very poor condition. One of the things that they wanted us to visit was a new government building in which I had no interest. I was interested in the little pedlars lining the side of the road, who were trying to sell us some souvenirs. I wanted to buy two souvenirs for two people, now grown up, who were born in the hospital when I was there and whose parents I was still in touch with. I wanted a little elephant and a paper knife which had been made in Sierra Leone. When I asked how much the elephant was I was told an exorbitant price and I said, 'No' and walked away. But I soon went back and said, 'How much now?' Though it had gone down a bit, to my way of thinking it was far far too high. I then reverted to a bit of pidgin and said, 'You be thief – I give you fifty shilling,' which was far too much really for what it was worth. He looked flabbergasted at this and I said, 'Wilberforce one time.' He laughed and said, 'This Madame, she knows this palaver,' and I got the elephant and the letter opener at a good price, but I gave him more than he asked me. The rest of the group from the ship asked me to bargain for them, but I said, 'No, do your own bargaining!' Before leaving the ship I had filled my bag with sweets and biscuits and had given them to the children when I was buying the elephant and the paper knife. Before the bus left for the ship there was a scuffle at the door and three Mammys demanded to get in and eventually did. They came up to me, kissed me and said, 'God bless you,' and left. There again I nearly cried.

8

Tour in Kenya

*(including my many Safari trips and
close encounters with the wildlife)*

I enjoyed my flight over part of East Africa to Nairobi – it was an RAF plane and I had a window seat. The hospital was very pleasant and in a lovely setting – the trees and flowers were beautiful and the bird life amazing. There was an earthquake one day, no one was hurt, but some of the equipment was damaged. One of my theatre orderlies seemed very unhappy – he had home troubles, I managed to help him and he was very grateful. We met again several times in different operating theatres, the last one in Berlin, where he was a fully qualified technician. He told me he was engaged and asked me to meet her which I did. She was a lovely German girl and they married and now live in Germany. They both visit me in my home when they come to England to see his relations and they are now grandparents – how time passes!

I took a day trip whilst on leave in Mombasa. I flew from Mombasa to Zanzibar and as soon as I got off the plane I was struck by the smell of the spices they grew there. My travelling companion, another QA, and I took a taxi tour around the island. The people, although poor, seemed happy and were very friendly. Zanzibar was quite unlike Africa at that time, mainly because it smelled so good, but also because it seemed very much behind the times there.

I was based in Nairobi at this time and at every opportunity I visited the national safari parks. I went around Lake Victoria on the SS *Usoga* and stayed at all the little ports around its perimeter. It took a week to complete the tour of the lake. We had a first class cabin on the ship but it was very basic. The first morning on deck was a great shock. The deck was crammed with people. There were little metal plates on deck for the passengers to make fires on which to cook. There were also quite an array of their animals with them and a small bus. It was quite a sight! I often wondered why the ship never caught fire but to my knowledge it never did. I very much enjoyed the trip although the wind on Lake Victoria was frequent and strong and my companion was seasick for much of the time.

Another time we took a train ride to Uganda up through the Rift Escarpment, which was stunning. I also visited the Queen Elizabeth Game Reserve in Uganda. The lodge we stayed at was very comfortable and we went out on several game runs. The mountains there were called 'The Mountains of the Moon' or 'En Zora Zora' by the locals and legend has it that this is where Solomon's treasure is buried.

I also visited Treetops where Princess Elizabeth was when she was informed of her father's death. This amazing place was built up in the trees with a veranda high above the ground. When you arrived it was traditional to be served tea on the veranda but as soon as the tea arrived so would the monkeys who ate it all – all part of the experience! The nearby watering hole was lit softly at night so that you could see the wildlife arrive to drink at night. We were out on the veranda after dinner to see what would come out when we heard an awful noise. Two Rhinos were fighting. We were informed that they would fight to the death and it would be a terrible sight. It also meant that in all probability any other animals would be deterred by the smell of blood from using the watering hole that night. However, the wind changed direction and we were very lucky to witness twenty-five elephants (including a baby) trekking down from Mount

Kenya. Many other nocturnal animals came to drink and the noise was fantastically loud. This carried on until daylight and I didn't get a wink of sleep. We left after breakfast.

I also visited Ambeselli National Park. The 'lodge' there was a tented affair open to the bush unlike any other lodge I had been to. On arrival it seemed deserted and the guide there told us that we were the only two people at that time. The whole compound had been hired by a group of Americans who had gone off into the bush for a few days to track chimpanzees, so we had the place to ourselves, or so it seemed …

Our tent was very comfortable but after dinner the fire was left to go out and a chap came along and turned out our kerosene lamp. It was very dark but we were tired and went straight to sleep. In the night we heard an almighty roaring noise the source of which came very close to our tent. We were scared out of our wits but it passed on and we eventually went back to sleep. Next morning at dawn a chap came back to our tent and relit our lamp and gave us each a cup of tea as we were going for an early morning game run. My friend needed a toilet so I looked out of the tent to see where it might be. I saw the back end of an elephant so my friend wouldn't go out. We 'excused' ourselves elsewhere! Later our guide showed us two lions that occasionally visited the camp cookhouse at night looking for leftover food. In daylight we saw them sitting a little way from the camp washing their faces rather like cats and looking harmless enough and the mystery was solved!

The first safari I actually went on was a package holiday from the UK, which I joined in Nairobi. Our first night's stop was in a Safari Lodge on the borders of Tanganyika. I was amazed at the luxury and enjoyed the night very much. Before starting off, we filled up the Safari vehicle at the petrol station. Standing by the roadside were two Masai tribesmen. They were in full tribal dress and one chap in our group liked taking photographs and was about to take the Masai's photograph when the guide told him that he must ask permission first. We did so and the Masai asked for 'five shillingee' each which seemed too much. The young chap asked us to distract them while he took a picture from the back of the truck. One of the Masai heard him and said in an accent straight from Oxford, 'No you don't, not unless you pay us.' Although they were true Masai they were actually being educated in Oxford and were on holiday just like us. This was the little scam they liked to play on the tourists!

Once I visited Gora Gora Crater whilst on leave. We had a guide drive us into the crater and show us around but once inside he seemed to get lost and couldn't find the way out. It was dusk by the time we found our way out and quite dark by the time we were returned to our camp. It was very dangerous to be out and about in the dark in those parts because of the wild animals.

When we got back to camp, the camp administrator was away leaving his wife in charge. We had been due back by 6pm and were now over an hour late. She had been so worried and was now in a bit of a state and quite cross with us. While we had been out a wounded Masai tribesman had been brought to her at the lodge and she was in quite a state about that too. He had been gored by a rhino and needed treatment and transportation to a hospital.

As a nurse, I offered to take a look at him and his wounds were extensive. He was lacerated from his chest to his abdomen. On closer inspection I could see that the wound had been packed with what smelled and looked like animal faeces to stop the bleeding. I was quite horrified but he seemed stable and he was able to talk. Another Masai translated for me and it appeared that he wasn't in too much pain either. I was very surprised, as the wounds looked life threatening and they had happened three days earlier. Transport was arranged and he was taken to the nearest hospital over ten miles away. About two weeks later I enquired about his welfare to be told that he was well and had been discharged. I was delighted.

I loved my time in Nairobi and we were all sorry when they got their independence and we had to leave.

9

Tour in Berlin (Predominantly nursing Hess)

After three years as the Senior Theatre Sister at the Cambridge Military Hospital, Aldershot, I was posted to Berlin. It was the time of the Cold War and entrance to Berlin was limited via 'the corridor' on an armed military train or by road monitored by our authorities on entry and exit. Also you could enter by a civilian aircraft. In the British sector there was only one airport but I was lucky as the RAF were stationed there and they took me.

Of the four occupying powers, three were in West Berlin and the Russians in East Berlin. I don't know about the Russians, but the Americans, French and British all had their own military hospitals. I became very friendly with the other two matrons and we had great times together. Sadly one has recently died.

The British Military Hospital was itself purpose built so that any war criminals in Spandau Prison had to be hospitalised there. As the cold war was on, there was a well equipped underground hospital built below the BMH hospital for emergency use even in the event of an atomic bomb. There were steps and lifts down from the main hospital, so that patients could be evacuated down there in any emergency. It was quite a large hospital but very pleasant to work in. The Officers' Mess was extremely comfortable – in fact we were a bit spoilt. Berlin itself was a very cultural city when it had been rebuilt, with the opera, ballet, concerts, museums and art galleries, so there was plenty to see and do. I had a very active social life.

I had been the matron for quite a short while and I was determined not to change things until I knew what I was doing. I had very mixed staff – there were QAs in training and the RAMC in training, German civilians and German trained nurses. They were all grumbling and I thought that four of them could come to my office and we would try to sort things out. I am afraid that I got very annoyed with their petty complaints. As I have said before, I have a bad temper, which I lost. On my desk was a glass top, which I thumped with a ruler and said a rude word. The glass smashed to pieces with a loud noise and I told the staff to leave the office. They did so in horror and haste! Outside an orderly was waiting to see the CO, who opened his office door and said, 'What's going on out there?' The orderly, knowing me very well said, 'They've overdone it; I knew she'd blow – they won't do that again!'

Having read Bird's *The Loneliest Man in the World* and an article in the *Telegraph*, I was reminded again of the time I had spent nursing Hess in the military hospital in Berlin in 1969. Parts of these pieces conflicted with my own experience of Hess and his care at that time, and so I feel compelled to put pen to paper on my impression of said patient.

The first time I had heard mention of Hess and Spandau prison, where he was held, was at the handover 'luncheon'. At this time in Berlin the French, British, and the Americans still occupied West Berlin and the Soviets controlled East Berlin. However, all four powers were involved in guarding Hess. They took it in turn to be in command and at each handover from one power to the next there was a luncheon in Spandau for all concerned. This usually consisted of four medical officers, four guard officers and a certain number of invited people such as officers' wives, nursing staff etc. This particular time it was the turn of the French to organise the luncheon (which is why I attended – they did the best spread!) At the time I thought it was rather paradoxical that we were all attending this lavish lunch and the main reason for all these people being together, namely Hess, was in a bare cell. I enjoyed it but my curiosity satisfied, I had no desire to go again.

On the afternoon that Hess was admitted to the B.M.H. the Admin Officer put his head round the door of my office and said 'It's on'. I had no idea what it meant but tried to look intelligent. I decided to investigate and soon found out that Hess was being transferred here from Spandau. The area he was to be held in was already occupied and I arranged for those patients to be moved. They all wanted to know why they were being moved and as it was all very hush-hush I told them that we had a violent psychiatric patient coming in and I didn't want them all to be disturbed by him. The area in which the patient was nursed was designed for such an occasion. There were grills over the windows and steel doors etc. We used it for medical patients and on the odd occasion for psychiatric patients as it was considered secure. The key to the window grill was kept locked away and only a select few members of staff had access to it.

Anyway, all was ready for our patient and I went to have one last look around before his arrival. The place was crawling with soldiers with guns. British, US, French and Russian were all there. I decided that this was no place for me and made myself busy elsewhere. The CO, a very charming man, decided it was time to meet my new patient and he took me to the room where the patient was being held. I was very curious to see this infamous man but when I met him I was horrified by what I saw. The room was full of guards and lying on the bed was this frail old man. He was clutching a very dirty, smelly, old blanket to his face. The CO said, 'Herr Hess, this is Matron. She will help to nurse you while you are here.' The blanket slowly descended from his face and Hess said, 'Good afternoon' and then he quickly drew the blanket up over his face again. I later learned that Hess was very fond of this blanket as it was the only thing he still possessed that had been his own.

Hess had his own warders: two US, two British, two French and two Russian. They were in constant attendance working in shifts two at a time. At the sight of this pathetic spectacle my nursing instinct took over and I organised for him to be bathed and made comfortable. I arranged for his blanket to be washed but it nearly fell to pieces.

I wondered if this frail old man was all he seemed to be and if he would be difficult to handle as his warders implied. I soon found out. As it turned out he could be very arrogant and rude and one morning on my visit I had occasion to tell him that he was '... a rude, bad and ungrateful old man'. He promptly turned his back to me, but on my next visit he apologised for his behaviour. He had a sense of humour though. He wanted a dressing gown so I set about finding something appropriate. One had to be careful, no belts were allowed in case he might hang himself. I brought him a dressing gown but apparently it was not to his liking. He said, 'The mini (*skirt*) might be in but I'd prefer a maxi.' I eventually found him something to suit.

He was also very fussy about his food and we tried to encourage him to drink more. I asked him if he liked milk and sugar in his tea and he replied that yes he did. Tea was provided. A few days later I asked him, 'How are you enjoying your tea?' He replied, 'Not so well, tea should be taken from good china, not thick army mugs.' I did get him a cup and saucer of fine china and took it in to him and announced, 'There's your *tassen mit unter tassen* – see how you like your tea now.' I had no more complaints about the tea.

I am afraid some of us did not stick rigidly to the rules and regulations surrounding Hess. In my view a patient is a patient no matter who or what he is. He wanted a picture for his wall as he said that lying in bed was depressing. I did find a picture of a town. It was an oil painting and therefore had no glass, which is just as well as he wasn't allowed glass. I took the picture to his room to a very cool reception. He told me 'take it away, your people destroyed that beautiful city'. I hadn't realised that it was a painting of Dresden! It was decided that a little occupational therapy might be a good thing and so I took him some 'Painting by Numbers'. Unfortunately it was met with scorn and treated with the contempt he felt it deserved.

We had a little joke about his health and how he was sleeping. He knew that he was 'news' and the press regularly reported about him. We liked to compare the press reports with reality. They often didn't tally and we would joke 'I see in the paper that you have not been sleeping too well' and he would reply 'But we know different!' Sometimes he would ask 'And how am I doing today?' and we'd have a little laugh.

All the time that he had been in Spandau, Hess refused visits from his wife and son as he felt too ashamed to let them see him in prison. However, he felt it was acceptable for them to visit him in the hospital and they did so on several occasions. The first time I was very concerned about him. I believe it was the first time he had seen his son since he was three years old. He was now a grown man. Hess was very nervous and we had to make sure he looked his best. He was to be reunited with his wife and son in a room that was usually occupied by the warders. After some delays they met. Hess was dressed in outdoor clothes. He was determined to look as dignified as possible.

One of his warders, a kindly man, used to take a portable TV into Hess so that he could watch football and some orchestral concerts. He was very fond of good music. His English was good and my German practically non-existent but we had quite a few conversations when I could get rid of the warders. On one occasion we discussed the birds, as it was very cold outside with deep snow. I told him how I liked to feed them in winter and he said that he used to do that too in Spandau. I told him I didn't like the cold and preferred the sunshine. Hess loved the snow as it reminded him of his 'beloved Bavaria'. He did not like the heat. He was telling me that he was born in Alexandria and I was explaining that I had served some time in the Canal Zone, when the warders returned and no more was said at that time. I had previously scolded the warders on the state of their room. I used this occasion to have another go at them about it. Although neither of them understood English they must have got the general idea from my voice and expression and the room was quickly cleaned up.

During my time in this post one particular incident stands out in my mind. Frau Hess arrived one afternoon accompanied by the usual retinue. This time she had a brown grip with her. Outside the secure area she said to me 'For him.' She was not allowed to take the grip into Hess's room and gave it to me. I didn't know what to do with it, as the guards had their eyes on me, and the grip. At the end of the visit I still had the grip and had to hand it back to Frau Hess, who was distressed. We were going down the corridor on her departure when I had an idea and said, 'Frau Hess, the toiletten?' She got the message and I said to the accompanying retinue, 'Gentlemen, this is one place you cannot escort Frau Hess to.' We both went into the toilet and undid the grip. It contained ten red roses (flowers were not allowed in Hess's room) I had tried once before to put a few spring flowers in his room but they were promptly removed by the Russians. We flushed the toilet and departed leaving the roses on the floor. I now had to get the roses to Hess. I thought 'boot-face' might do the trick. I alerted the RAMC Sergeant on duty that I needed a vase of water and the key to the grill over Hess's window. On my evening visit I marched in with my best cross expression and blasted all and sundry about the state of the place etc. I had my long corridor cape on with the roses hidden within. The Sergeant had done his stuff. The grill was unlocked with a vase of water put behind it. I put the roses in and we locked the grill and conveniently mislaid the key. I said to Hess, who was a bit confused by these goings on, that they were from his wife. He was delighted. I left smartly.

Several days later he said when the CO and myself were on our morning visit that he had written to his wife to say he had had a dream that was rather strange as he thought they were on their honeymoon and he had bought her ten red roses. As his letters were censored, he hoped this would escape their notice and that his wife would understand that he had received the roses.

The press had speculated that this man was not Hess as it was known that Hess had been wounded in World War I yet this prisoner did not have any scars. However in my experience scars can fade. If this man was not Hess I cannot think why he allowed himself to be incarcerated for all those years and for what purpose. If he was Hess, no doubt he had committed many crimes and I am old enough to have experienced the horror of the war first-hand but whatever this man's crimes, it could have done no harm to show him some humanity.

As he spent Christmas in hospital we thought we would see if we could give him a bit of Christmas cheer. The Russians didn't think so. I had asked if we could relax the routine a little, but this was refused. The presents Frau Hess had sent were examined by the Russians and disposed of. He was allowed to have none of them.

I thought as we were going to have a Father Christmas it would cheer the old man if he could be visited by him and be given a little gift. We thought soap would be harmless. This was frowned on by the Russians and the usual 'Gnet' was the answer when this was suggested. Nurses can often be devious where their patient is concerned. Father Christmas was in fact the RAMC sergeant who was responsible for Hess's nursing. As he was on duty Christmas Day at lunchtime, there was no reason to ask how he should be dressed so Hess did have Father Christmas visit him. He also stayed for lunch and I think a little bottle of wine was produced and consumed by both patient and Father Christmas. Soap was also produced from Father Christmas's pocket. I was off duty on Christmas Eve, my 2 i/c being on duty. It is the custom for staff to sing carols round the wards and it was decided that Hess should not be forgotten. *Silent Night* was sung outside his room, the steel door being ajar for this purpose. I am told the old man wept.

His discharge from hospital was kept quiet and I was only told on the morning of his departure that he was to return to Spandau that day. He was very upset and tried to talk to me but the British warder at the time (the nasty one) would not allow this. They both got very angry, both speaking in German. I thought it best to leave saying to Hess not to get upset. I had to help escort him to the ambulance and we did get a few minutes together without interruption. The old man held my hand and said, 'thank you for being kind to me, and for being polite.' Who are we to judge, and if these lines give the impression that one doesn't realise the enormity of the crime of the Nazi regime, it is not intended to be so. All I know about our patient was that he was a sick, frightened old man. From the nursing angle he wasn't even senile and certainly didn't strike me as being insane, as the articles I have read about him seem to imply.

When I was stationed in Berlin I liked to go into the East to see the Opera. I preferred the Opera House there and the cast seemed younger and more the part. Being the occupying force we could cross easily into the East through Checkpoint Charlie so long as we had on our uniform. The Matron-in-Chief for the QAs came to visit and we took her to see the Opera in East Berlin. She wore full military evening dress and she was very attractive anyway and she made quite a stir amongst the East Berlin audience. They had never seen anything like it and it was actually mentioned in their newspaper as if she was some kind of celebrity. I felt proud of the QAs at that moment.

When in East Berlin you weren't allowed to buy anything (you weren't allowed to support their economy). However, I liked their crystal glass and many times brought back a few pieces, mostly wine glasses. Everybody did it and no one ever checked. We pretty much came and went in East Berlin as we wished.

I spent three years in the BMH Berlin and was very sorry to leave this posting.

Many years later the spectre of Hess rose again. My QA friend since Malta, Barbara Norman, had a relative in the Diplomatic Corps and he was retiring. We were going to house-sit for him while he took his wife on holiday. Just before his departure he held a large luncheon party. At this time Hess was front page news again as he had allegedly hanged himself. The conversation at the luncheon was mainly about Hess. Barbara said, 'Ask Rosemary – she nursed him.' Not thinking, I said, 'I don't understand how a feeble old man could hang himself without help.' I didn't think any more of it but shortly after the party I received three anonymous telephone calls from people saying they had heard that I had nursed Hess and they wanted me to tell them more about it. I wouldn't be drawn on the subject and replied that I had only nursed him, nothing more. Six months after that I received a call from a Detective Inspector from New Scotland Yard.

I thought it was one of my friends playing a prank on me and said, 'Pull the other one!' However, it wasn't a joke, this was serious. Hess's son had contacted the authorities to say that there was a woman by the name of Sutton who was telling people that Hess could not have hanged himself. Apparently Hess's son was having trouble believing it too. I explained to the DI that I had received three anonymous phone calls (probably journalists) but that I had disclosed nothing. The DI was very concerned about this and asked that if they contacted me again I should try to find out their identity and pass the information on to him. I didn't receive any more calls but I learned from this experience to be very careful about what I say in company! It also brought it back to me that although I had viewed Hess as an old man who happened to be my patient for a while, the rest of the world never tired of the Hess enigma even to this day.

10

Marjorie

My very dear friend Marjorie has been such a big part of my life that I should explain a bit about her. We first met when I lived in Merrow near Guildford as a child. We went to school together and, although Marjorie was five years younger than I, she only lived a few houses down from me and we walked to school together most days. When I joined the Army we kept in touch by letter and I would visit her when I was on leave back home. She married a policeman but I was on tour overseas at the time. I had never thought much of this chap and in time he abandoned Marjorie and her two young children for another woman. Back then this type of behaviour was not acceptable in the police force and he was discharged. As he and Marjorie had lived in police accommodation, Marjorie then lost her home and was forced to move in with her mother. Again I was abroad when this all happened and the first I knew was when Marjorie wrote to me telling me to send all future mail to her mother's address. Unfortunately it was very cramped at her mother's house, not helped by the fact that Marjorie's brother and his new wife were also living there. Marjorie tried to get her own place but in those days very little assistance was available for a woman in her position.

I also wanted to get a place of my own to return to when I was home on leave. I wasn't getting on too well with my stepmother, although she and my father were very happy together. My father died at the age of 93 and she died five years later. Anyway, each time I was home I would visit all of the estate agents in Godalming (near Guildford) to see what they had on offer. In time they got to know me quite well. When Marjorie's predicament became clear I doubled my efforts to secure a home for both of us. The idea was that she could look after the house when I was on tour. Home on leave again I went to the estate agents in Godalming desperate to find something. This time they had only two properties available to buy in the area. One was too expensive and the other was Bargate House. The estate agent wasn't too hopeful about it and explained that it was in a bit of a state but I insisted that I look at it and so they gave me the keys and pointed me in the general direction. Although it was very neglected I liked it. It was already divided into two flats and the rooms were a good size. I bought the house with the help of a council mortgage and then promptly left for Germany. Marjorie was left with the task of making the house habitable on her own. She worked like a Trojan and with some help from my father in the garden she made the place good. The man from the council thought I was mad. He didn't think two women could fix up such a badly neglected house. He took it all back when he saw the transformation.

When we bought our new home Marjorie's two children, Christine and Trisha, were seven and two years old. They grew up in this house and although they each have now made their own way in life they still visit and always feel like they are returning home. Both Trisha and Christine are married. Christine, a Chartered Accountant with two daughters and a son, is married to an Austrian and lives in Austria. Trisha is a podiatrist and is married to a Czech. They live together with their daughter in Hove, East Sussex.

I feel very lucky that throughout my life I have had many good friends but in particular Marjorie has been my closest friend and support from childhood and throughout my life to the present day. She has been like my family and I feel thankful for that.

11

WRAC Centre Guildford

My last posting was to the WRAC Centre in Guildford where I was in charge of the Medical Centre. At that time every few weeks, a large number of young girls arrived for their six-week Basic Training. It was a totally different situation to what I had been used to. It took me time to adjust to being responsible for an all-female staff, as all my previous experience was with men and patients. I was very sad to have to retire at fifty-five years old. However, I was offered an extension to the Guildford posting as a retired re-employed officer. I finally retired aged sixty-five. My father was in his nineties and sick and needed me near home.

While I was at the WRAC Centre in Guildford, the IRA were very active and we had a lot of bomb scares. I helped to nurse some of the WRAC girls who were injured and very distressed by the bombing of the pub in Guildford as they were in the pub at the time of the bombing. Sadly there was loss of life.

I was able to get home very often as I was living in Godalming at this time. It was during my time in Guildford, that I received the news that I had been awarded the Associate of the Royal Red Cross medal, which is awarded for special nursing service. When I was told that I was to receive this I was asked who I would like to present it to me. I asked for the Queen Mother and she presented it to me at a ceremony at Buckingham Palace. I could not help but be sad that my beloved father had not lived to see this day. He had died six months earlier.

12

Retirement

When I retired from the Army in the 1980s I spent most of my gratuity on a three-month World Cruise. In addition to seeing the world I used this opportunity to catch up with friends all over the world. When we stopped for one night in San Francisco I stayed over with a friend. She had been the Matron of one of the hospitals in Berlin where we became good friends. When we stopped off in Hawaii I visited with an old ex-Army boyfriend who had moved there when he retired. As we crossed the Pacific we stopped off at a number of islands which were absolutely beautiful. Then when we got to Australia some good friends, one of whom had been my uncle's godson, met me off the ship at Sydney. We had lunch at the Opera House and had a wonderful time. In Hong Kong, we stopped for two nights and it was there that Marjorie joined me for the rest of the cruise. From there we took a trip into China together. This trip was very enlightening for us both. While there we had a very interesting (but not very appetising) lunch. We called into Port Saffiga on the Red Sea in Egypt. From there we took a trip into the Valley of the Kings. We crossed the desert by coach but there were no facilities onboard or by the roadside. When we stopped for a comfort break, this meant *al fresco* toilet with the men on one side of the coach and women on the other. We visited the tomb of Tutankhamun. I found this fascinating and something I shall never forget. On previous cruises I had been to the museum in Cairo and had seen all of his artefacts and treasures but the tomb had all the paintings on the walls. You could see where the sarcophagus had been and it was all so colourful and stunning.

We made a stop in Morocco and had a day trip to Marrakech. I enjoyed it very much and we visited the souk and bought a little alabaster Nefertiti ornament as I'd previously seen an original sculpture in a museum in Berlin. I haggled for the ornament, using skills I had developed while working in Egypt. Eventually I spoke to the shopkeeper in Arabic and told him what I thought it was worth and he was so taken aback, he laughed and agreed to my price. He got his own back though by charging my friend Marjorie the full price. She was too embarrassed to haggle.

I enjoyed that cruise so much that when it was time to leave I got quite emotional. I had made many friends on board the ship. One chap in particular who was my partner for the quizzes became a close friend and we still keep in touch.

I had always travelled throughout my working life and loved it so much that I've continued to see the world by taking cruises every year. Marjorie has accompanied me on many occasions. My favourite ship was the *Canberra*. This ship became famous as she had been commissioned by the Army during the Falklands War, and along with many others, I was very saddened when she was eventually scrapped. Even now I still manage to take one cruise a year and this year I visited the Fjords in Norway. I only ever travel on P&O ships.

Now at the ripe old age of ninety I look back on all the things I have done and all the places I have been to and my memories are a great solace and keep me young.